AWAKEN THE MIGHTY
WARRIOR

SPIRITUAL BOOT CAMP AND TRAINING FOR THE END TIME BELIEVER

BY SCOTTI BISCOSSI

Copyright © 2016 by Scotti Biscossi

Awaken The Mighty Warrior
Spiritual Boot Camp And Training For The End Tme Believer
by Scotti Biscossi

Printed in the United States of America.

Edited by Xulon Press

ISBN 9781498469982

All rights reserved solely by the author. The author guarantees all contents are original and do not infringe upon the legal rights of any other person or work. No part of this book may be reproduced in any form without the permission of the author. The views expressed in this book are not necessarily those of the publisher.

Scripture quotations taken from the New International Version (NIV). Copyright © 1973, 1978, 1984, 2011 by Biblica, Inc.™. Used by permission. All rights reserved.

Scripture quotations taken from the New King James Version (NKJV). Copyright © 1979, 1980, 1982 by Thomas Nelson, Inc. Used by permission. All rights reserved.

www.xulonpress.com

TABLE OF CONTENTS

Dedication vii
Introduction ix

Chapter 1 13
Chapter 2 17
Chapter 3: The Armor Of The Lord 29
Chapter 4: The Gates 61
Chapter 5: Old Versus New Dispensation What Does
    That Mean? 71
Chapter 6: Hopelessness And Depression 77
Chapter 7: Deception And The Spirit Of Jezebel 83
Chapter 8: Captured And Tortured 89
Chapter 9: Becoming Fluent In Your Spirit Language: Your
    Spiritual Grenade 93

Work Book 97
Resources 101

DEDICATION

Dedicated to my Lord and Savior who has brought me through the many battles I have faced on this journey of faith. To my husband, who has encouraged and supported me in every endeavor involving ministry or my life. To my dear prayer partners and closest faith friends, Pinky Person and Karen Stouse, who have prayed and stood with me oh-so-many times in prayer and believed God had a special calling in mind for me. To my friends Susan Lipsitt and Doris Pinhack, and Charlie Brogan who were there for me in some of the darkest hours of my life. To my daughter who has always been my biggest cheerleader. To all those ministers and leaders especially Mike and Cindy Redmon, Rose Lee who believed in me and prayed and encouraged me to go forward in the Lord's calling. Finally, to my daughters Michelle and Stephanie, and my friend Debbie Freese who financially supported me, this book is written with you in mind. One day we may no longer be here, but this book will always be there for you. Then as you read it, you will remember the words we spoke into your lives to encourage and strengthen you for the journey ahead. May you continue your walk with the Savior and be the voice that carries on the message of the Gospel of Yeshua.

> *Psalm 45:1: "My heart is stirred by a noble theme as I recite my verses for the King; my tongue is the pen of a skillful writer."*

> *Jude vs. 3: "Beloved, when I gave all diligence to write unto you of the common salvation it was needful for me to write unto you and exhort you that ye should earnestly contend for the faith which was once delivered unto the saints."*

Thank you, Karen for this prophetic word you gave me. It gave me strength as I embarked on writing this book.

INTRODUCTION

Ephesians 4:11-16

"It was HE who gave some to be apostles, some to be prophets, some to be evangelists and to some to be pastors and teachers, to prepare God's people for works of service, so that the body of Christ may be built up until we all reach unity in the faith and in the knowledge of the Son of God and become MATURE, attaining to the whole measure of the fullness of Christ. Then we will no longer be infants, tossed back and forth by the waves, and blown here and there by every wind of doctrine and by the cunning and craftiness of men in their deceitful scheming. Instead speaking the truth in love, we will in all things grow up into him who is the Head, that is, CHRIST. From him the whole body, joined and held together by every supporting ligament grows and builds itself up in love, as each part does its work."

My prayer is that this book will equip the saints with the knowledge to fight courageously, fully suited, in the battles they will face in the future. Over the last couple of years, I have been honored and blessed to have had the opportunity to minister to so many the gospel of Yeshua/Jesus Christ. I did not choose this path; I was very comfortable singing and sitting in congregation hearing the Word and doing my little part. But when the Savior calls, he beckons like a lover, and we cannot resist his presence.

The day Donnivan Hickman came into my life, I was so confused. I remember asking God for a man to share my life with, but I was very certain I said, "But please don't make me a pastor's wife. You know how I am, and I really don't want to fail you, and surely I would." Twenty years later, Donnivan Hickman would ask me (after our first date by the way) to pray about being a pastor's wife, and I froze. This wasn't what **I** wanted; this was a big responsibility. I really didn't want to be the person who jointly with my husband would be responsible for the sheep and goats in the congregations.

But God showed Donnie how to love me; he showed me a love I had never known before. It was the love that Christ showed the church by giving his life for our redemption. I began to observe this love as if I were viewing a movie. There were times when he would just hold my face and say, "Do you know how much I love you?" And in all honesty, all I could do was look into his eyes and realize how foreign it was to know this kind of love. No one had ever had such intensity and sincerity of love for me like this man. Needless to say, as I prayed over the coming months, "Lord is this the one?" I could hardly believe God would or even could use a damaged vessel like me.

Introduction

Then I attended a woman's conference. The evangelist was Ellen Coon, a mighty woman of God. I will never forget her coming and pulling me out of my seat which was way in the back of the church during the conference. She didn't know me nor did I know her, but I could feel the anointing that day. She prophesied over me, and I wish I could remember all she said, but I do recall some. She said, "You have been sitting in the back too long, you have been called to ministry. Don't worry about what you can and cannot do; He will equip you for the job. You have been called out. He has led you through many obstacles to get here, and many times you thought your life was useless, but he was making you a warrior. You are a fighter, and your knowledge is needed in this day. Today is the day of decision ... Say YES." There was ever so much more, but that day I said, "Yes, Lord I am willing; here I am if you can use me."

As I was in the Spirit, it was like seeing a video of the things I had come through. Truly, there were things that even I had forgotten. As the pictures rolled, his voice was clear to me..."These were all the enemy's attempts at destroying you and your faith, but I used each one to prepare you for the work you will do. You see, now you can understand the pain and suffering of my people, and I will use you to teach them a warrior spirit. For these are the last days and they will be perilous indeed. Many will fall away, but you, my daughter, my "**Princess Warrior**", will have a voice that will ring out like none other, and when you do, it will break chains. You are *fierce* because you know what the enemy looks like. You will uncover

Satan's deceptions in those who are presently in the fight but are young in the faith and not as strong as you. "Again, so much more was spoken, but that is what I remember most.

Since that day, I have watched as the sheep are maimed by the circumstances of life, wandering around being tossed about like rag dolls by the enemy because they have yet to learn to stand firm and trust God. I began seeing how unequipped the saints were when it came to adversity, trials, temptations, and sickness. That is the purpose of this book. It is all the Lord has shown me in the Spirit but also all the experiences that have contributed to my own maturity. May the God of Israel be pleased and praised with this manual.

CHAPTER 1

I was in my prayer closet on Monday June 1, 2015, wondering what God had planned for my husband Donnie and I as we stepped out into ministry. He had heard from the Lord while I was away that it was time to leave his assistant pastoral position at the church we were attending and begin a new work. As his wife, I always want to be cautious about such decisions but trusted that this was the will of God. I told the Lord I was ready but felt very unequipped, but as they say, he does not call the equipped, He equips the called. I trust the Lord will lead and teach us in exactly what He wants us to do. That morning as I sat quietly praying, I heard that still small voice say, "I want you to write a book." I thought, "I can't write a book. I don't think I am smart enough nor do I have a message to give." But again I heard, "I want you to write a book, don't worry what it is about I will give you the message as you write." So here I am writing at my computer, still curious how this will all be, but trusting the Lord to show me exactly what He wants to tell the Church.

The Sunday we shared our final service, I found it much more difficult than I thought it would be. I looked around at the many people we had counseled and helped during their darkest hours. I remember each person's testimony of deliverance as they began to grow in the Lord and how fast some of them grew in the months that had passed. I realized we had a bond—that bond was the love of the Savior that brought us out, each one of us saved in the nick of time. Tears falling, many of them came and hugged and loved on us, and we could feel the heartstrings tugging. One little girl, who really wasn't a little girl except to me, said she was going to miss me because when she needed to be loved on, she would come sit on my lap and I would love on her and pray with her. I cried as I realized this was the heart of the father in me. How I wanted her to succeed in her walk and how I knew the enemy wanted to take her out. But looking at her that Sunday made me so happy because I could see the growth in her, I saw the struggles and how she hung on at times for dear life, sometimes even wanting to give up. She said that she appreciated the fact that I wouldn't let her give up. She was right I wouldn't, because I loved her enough to chase her down when she was ready to quit and speak life into her.

Reinhard Bonnke said in his book, "I want to plunder Hell to populate Heaven." I will never forget that and I live by that motto. She is developing into a powerful woman of God and will be doing a ton of plundering herself. Her growth was quick and heavy, and I realized early on how many of our young people were growing so

Chapter 1

fast. Faster than ever before, and it entered my spirit that the Lord was speeding up the clock because time was so much shorter than we even were aware. They needed to be equipped for battles they had never faced, and yet how were we to teach them all that we took years to learn? I could only pray and depend on the Lord to show me as we walked along. I asked what the immediate needs were and hoped to address those first. Armor and learning why it is so important to wear it all the time should be where we begin. Then on to artillery that would blow the enemy right out of this world. And so that is exactly what I began to do. Each person is an individual; each person has their own journey filled with obstacles and battles, distractions and temptations, but first we have got to get our basic battle garments on.

My journey was not easy, and I think most of us can recall the many things we endured for the sake of the Gospel, but it has been worth it all. I can tell you that Yeshua (Jesus) is alive and well and performing miracles, signs, and wonders in this day. We, the true believers, must become readied for the battles that are coming. We haven't seen anything yet, and if you think the battles you have fought to date were hard, they will be nothing in comparison to the persecution of the believer to come.

So let us begin... ARE YOU READY FOR THE BATTLE?

CHAPTER 2

One of the things I have noticed over the years is how new converts are guided following their salvation. What I realized is that more often than not, we give them a bible, a bit of guidance, and off they go. This is what God showed me about that.

I was in the Marine Corp, and I learned preparedness, persistence, and discernment of not only my surroundings but also the enemy. It is from this place God began to speak to me about the Church. In the beginning, one must commit to the Marines. They go down to the recruiter's office and say, "I want to join and serve." This looks much like salvation in the primary stages. Our hearts are pricked by the Holy Spirit, and we come to the place of commitment and say, "I want Yeshua to be Lord of my life. I repent of my sins and commit my life to living in service to Him."

Now for many people, this is where it ends. Are they saved? The word of God says yes they are. *Romans 10:9 says, "If you declare with your mouth that Jesus is Lord, and believe in your heart that God raised him from the dead, you will be saved."* But is that all there is?

Certainly not, for Paul goes on to say in Romans 12 that once salvation is received and *"in view of that mercy" we should offer our bodies as living sacrifices, holy and pleasing to God. This is our spiritual act of worship.*

Let us look at what it is like being a soldier. Imagine signing up for a military service to be a soldier in the United States Marine Corps. You see, as a Marine soldier, once you sign those papers, you belong to the Marine Corps, and they will remind you of that daily. The very first thing that happens is that you get a uniform, haircut, boots, and a manual. The haircut for the men is a complete shaved head; for the women, it is a boy cut. The objective is to show each individual that they are all alike; no one person is greater than another. This is the beginning of your training. They don't care how much you know, how good you are, or what you think of yourself. You are nothing until they make you something. They do that by taking away **YOUR** pride first, and then they will begin to instill a **pride for the Corps**.

The spiritual warrior's process is no different. He is saved by grace just like everyone else; he is given a uniform, boots, and a bible. God begins to strip away all the evil that lurks within us, especially **our pride**, because it cannot coexist with the Holy Spirit which will unveil all the sin and pride that is within us. Therefore, it must go. Doesn't matter how well you sing, or how well you can preach or do anything in the church for that matter. Pride will be the first to go. Sometimes He will even use other Christians to tear that out of us because pride is the first place the enemy goes to take you

Chapter 2

down. From the beginning of time, it was pride that brought evil to this world.

Eve, who was beguiled by the serpent to believe she will not surely die, looks at the fruit and tells the serpent, "But God said we may eat fruit from the trees in the garden but not of the tree in the middle of the garden, and you must not touch it or you will die." First of all, she embellished what God said. Did God say she couldn't touch it? No!!! He said you cannot eat it, and if you do, you will know the difference between good and evil and you will surely die. Here is another example of trying to embellish what God says. We need to obey his directives without question and without embellishment.

I have always pondered her response. Was she not listening or did she get all confused? Here is the fact—she saw the fruit was pleasing to the eye, and it was edible, and the bible says she took it and ate it. Often the enemy will use something or someone that is pleasing to the eye. People of God, don't fall for that; be on guard. So many of us have fallen beneath that spell, and it always leads to destruction and separation from God. So remember just because it looks good doesn't mean it is. Now Adam, who was standing close by because the bible says she hands it to Adam to taste, also heard this whole conversation and doesn't interrupt her and doesn't drag her away before she sins. Interesting, right? In fact, this is just my opinion, but I think Adam stood there and allowed her to go ahead and eat to see if she really would die. When she didn't, I think he thought it was okay to taste also. But what Adam didn't know was that he was the Head of His wife; he was supposed to protect her.

So although she sins, the curse doesn't fall until Adam eats the fruit and batta bing batta boom, suddenly both their eyes are opened. A single bite of sin can separate you from the love and fellowship of the Lord. PRIDE IS THE NUMBER ONE KILLER OF ALL SAINTS. We can show this with many others, King Saul, the magician Simon who thought he could buy the Holy Spirit. People listen, PRIDE will dull your hearing to the Lord and thus lead you into deception and wrong doctrine because the enemy loves to use pride. Why? Because it is human nature to be someone or accomplish something or be seen as important, and when people begin to be lifted up instead of the Holy One of Israel, PRIDE WILL TAKE OVER. Often we are not even aware how far into pride a person is until it's too late. Once there, destruction and death are inevitable. I want to add here that even the very elect fall prey to pride. You need only look to the great men of God that were seduced by the spirit of Pride.

It is for this reason I tell people constantly, do not follow a man of God. He is just a man and will fail you. Only Yeshua is perfect and our example, so let us keep our eyes on Him. Stop worshipping pastors, evangelists, and prophets, and all you leaders in these positions better tell them to worship God and God alone lest YOU fall. Harsh perhaps, but remember something—one day you as leaders will have to answer for all those sheep that ended up maimed and

Chapter 2

bruised because you didn't keep the focus on Yeshua and started basking in the glory that only belongs to Him. I wouldn't want to be in your shoes on the day of judgment, and make no mistake—there will come that day. I am always amazed by pastors who judge their congregations by the numbers or offerings they are amassing rather than the number of souls saved, healed or delivered. Let's get back to what God intended the church body to be. Not a building or group, but an outreach for salvation and eternity. That's a simple word of caution to those who will have an ear to hear.

So the first thing God has to do is remove pride. How? He gives us a garment of white for our sinful, trashy clothes when we repent. He covers us in the blood, and we are given the Holy Spirit as part of our uniform. It is the single most important piece of equipment you will carry, and it must be protected. God then gives us armor, and finally He gives us the manual—THE BIBLE. As we read, the Spirit illuminates and directs and changes us to become loyal soldiers in the Army of the Lord. The bible becomes our survival manual. If we do not read and truly follow it, we will find that the enemy will have more success in defeating us. You have to know the Word, because Satan knows the Word and will twist it so whatever sin you are faced with will look pleasing to the eye. He will give you a dozen reasons why it's okay to do or live as you do. KNOW THE WORD.

Next, in the Marine Corps, we find ourselves being instructed in the basics of warfare—what do you do when you get captured, how do you endure the gas chamber, how to overcome obstacles?

Learning the parts of the weapon and reciting the creed—this is my rifle this is my life. It is pretty intense, and I will share it for the sake of information. Note: This creed is going to shock some of you, but please read on as the Lord showed me His creed for us.

RIFLE CREED

This is my rifle. There are many like it, but this one is mine.

My rifle is my best friend. It is my life. I must master it as I must master my life. My rifle, without me, is useless. Without my rifle, I am useless. I must fire my rifle true. I must shoot straighter than my enemy who is trying to kill me. I must shoot him before he shoots me. I WILL...

My rifle and I know that what counts in this war is not the rounds we fire, the noise of our burst, nor the smoke we make. We know that it is the hits that count. WE WILL HIT...

My rifle is human, even as I, because it is my life. Thus, I will learn it as a brother. I will learn its weaknesses, its strength, its parts, its accessories, its sights, and its barrel. I will ever guard it against the ravages of weather and damage as I will ever guard my legs, my arms, my eyes, and my heart against damage. I will keep my rifle clean and ready. We will become part of each other. WE WILL...

Before God, I swear this creed. My rifle and myself are the defenders of my country. We are the masters of our enemy. WE ARE

Chapter 2

THE SAVIORS OF OUR LIVES. So be it, until victory is America's and there is no enemy, but peace.

Yes, that is intense and it is meant to be because when you are in a battle, your split second delay could cost lives. The soldiers who successfully complete boot camp are so well versed in their rifle it has become part of them. They can literally take apart and put back together their rifles while blindfolded. I guess you really have to know your weapon well to do that. This is true in the spiritual realm as well.

Here is what God gave me this morning about our Holy Spirit Creed.

HOLY SPIRIT CREED

This is the Holy Spirit in me. Many have it but few use it properly, but God has given this measure to me and He is mine.

The Holy Spirit is my best friend. He was sent by Yeshua to comfort and lead me. He is my life. I must master the quiet and my life so that I can hear His voice.

The Holy Spirit without a willing vessel cannot reach the world. He needs me to speak forth Truth as a willing vessel.

Without the Holy Spirit, I am useless, a broken vessel of little use, and in some cases totally dysfunctional. I must hold on to the Bow of Truth firmly and shoot the arrows of Salvation true by allowing the God of Israel to stretch me through trials.

I must be more accurate than the enemy who is trying to kill me and God's people.

I must shoot the enemy before he shoots me because you know he is aiming for my weakness.

I will shoot true by the Holy Spirit.

The Holy Spirit and I know what counts in a war is not the quantity of arrows shot out, not the noise you create in doing so as in songs we sing, but it is the number of direct hits by His Spirit we make, and WE WILL HIT ACCURATELY.

The Holy Spirit is part of me and therefore goes before me. He is my life. I will learn more about the Holy Spirit and how it works in me through the Word of God until the Holy Spirit is so entrenched and entwined within me that I no longer exist, but Christ is all you see.

I will learn my weaknesses and how He makes me strong to stand against the wiles of the enemy. I will learn to walk, talk, and act in a way that is in accordance with the Spirit.

I will guard my eyes and ears and tongue from all the worldly ravages of sin in this life to protect the power of the Holy Spirit in me.

I will keep my temple clean and ready for battle at all times.

Before God, I pledge this creed. THAT WE ARE THE DEFENDERS OF THE FAITH, WE ARE THE MASTERS OVER THE ENEMY BY THE POWER OF THE HOLY SPIRIT AND OUR MISSION IS SALVATION FOR ALL.

As we begin to read the Word, it becomes part of us and a sword of military force. When we are under attack we will speak it forth instantly. Without it, you will die. You must know it. It must be your life. You are one in the Spirit with the Holy One of Israel.

So the creed of the Bible is:

MY BIBLE CREED

This is my bible. It is my life. Without it, I am weak and ineffective.

With the words from this bible, I will be equipped to shoot the enemy, shoot straight, shoot true, and I will shoot—make no mistake about that. I will become so familiar with the words contained in this bible that when the enemy attacks, the first words out of my mouth will be the Word of God. When the enemy attacks my fellow soldiers, I will raise this Word as a standard against the enemy dragging my injured comrades back to medivac where they can receive the balm of Gilead poured over their wounds. I will snatch them from the very gates of Hell for the sake of the Gospel.

My fellow soldiers and I will be one in unity knowing that revival will come and victory will be ours when each of us is revived by the grace of God. When having done all, we will stand with one another until that day He returns and delivers us to our reward. May my heart remain always steady, ready, and soft. Let the Spirit work on my life through the Word of God till He calls me Home, and until that day, may I be the **WARRIOR** of the Gospel of Yeshua Messiah that He has called me to.

Now the real training begins—boot camp. No one likes boot camp; it hurts. I remember blisters the size of baseballs, muscles so sore I thought I couldn't even get out of my bunk. Running around like chickens all the time. Obstacle courses that made grown men as well as women cry. Running in foul weather, wet to the core, cold and hungry, and if you lagged behind, there was a drill instructor with a bat in hand threatening you. C rations which looked like cat food and (in my opinion) were seriously inedible, so you only ate the crackers and chocolate. But each test, each obstacle, each 20 mile hike was instilling in us a fearlessness. There wasn't anything that we didn't think we could do coming out of that. We had a pride, but it wasn't in ourselves; it was in the Corps and the training.

So it is with spiritual boot camp. No one likes having our faults exposed for all to see. Looking so raw, it's downright ugly. Times when you sat at the altar and cried till your face was black because your mascara ran, or eyes so blood shot from crying your face was actually distorted. It is here our pride is removed as we confess to one another our failures. The pain of sin goes deep. So does the pain of hate that you feel due to unforgiveness. But God has a plan. That plan is for your good, the bible says.

So first remove all the hate, all the sin, all the unforgiveness, all the pain of the past. Sometimes this is worse than a 20 mile hike in the rain. It is painful truly painful. We will want to give up sometimes because it is so painful. But there are always saints around who have been there, done that, and are ready to jerk you up by your boot straps and slap you up side your face and say, "Hey, what are you believing? Whose report you gonna believe? Stop whining get back in the battle. You can do it. I am right here beside you; we will stand together until victory is achieved."

Once all that garbage is gone, although I don't think that God ever stops working on that stuff because it goes so deep sometimes that it can be years later and still God is uncovering deep pains or disappointments. But those of us who have been in the battle like so many veterans in the corps, we aren't afraid of the enemy anymore because we know what he looks like and we can save lives by telling and instructing and leading the new boots into battle. So we will endure training by the grace of God.

Then one day we find ourselves graduating and going to battle. Now we get our protective gear for the battle. Helmets are first on the list, then flak jackets, extra socks, and new boots. Yeah, we are ready now. Show me my spiritual gear and let's get in the battle. Are you really ready?

"You therefore must endure hardship as a good soldier of Jesus Christ. No one engaged in warfare entangles himself with the affairs of this life, that he may please him who enlisted him as a soldier" (2 Timothy 2:3, 4, NKJV).

Chapter 3

THE ARMOR OF THE LORD

Ephesians 6:10-20

"*Finally, my brethren, be strong in the Lord, and in the power of his might.*

Put on the whole armor of God that ye may be able to stand against the wiles of the devil.

For we wrestle not against flesh and blood, but against principalities, against powers, against the rulers of the darkness of this world, against spiritual wickedness in high places.

Wherefore take unto you the whole armor of God that ye may be able to withstand in the evil day, and having done all, to stand.

Stand therefore, having your loins girt about with truth, and having on the breastplate of righteousness;

And your feet shod with the preparation of the gospel of peace;

Above all, taking the shield of faith, wherewith ye shall be able to quench all the fiery darts of the wicked.

And take the helmet of salvation, and the sword of the Spirit, which is the word of God:

Praying always with all prayer and supplication in the Spirit, and watching thereunto with all perseverance and supplication for all saints;

And for me, that utterance may be given unto me, that I may open my mouth boldly, to make known the mystery of the gospel, For which I am an ambassador in bonds: that therein I may speak boldly, as I ought to speak"

2 Corinthians 10:3-6 NIV

" For though we live in the world, we do not wage war as the world does. 4 The weapons we fight with are not the weapons of the world. On the contrary, they have divine power to demolish strongholds. 5 We demolish arguments and every pretension that sets itself up against the knowledge of God, and we take captive every thought to make it obedient to Christ. 6 And we will be ready to punish every act of disobedience, once your obedience is complete."

BELT

The first article of clothing in the armor is the **BELT OF TRUTH**. Armor is not a new idea. In fact, we can go back into scripture and see verses where armor is discussed. We see in 1

Samuel, David tried to wear the armor of Saul but one cannot wear another's armor. In 1 Chronicles, Saul and his sons are killed and the Philistines strip them of their armor, it says as an act of humiliation and presentation to their idols and gods. Isaiah and Ezekial talked about armor as well. So that tells us armor was an important part of the scriptures even in the Old Testament.

What was the purpose of the belt? Its primary purpose was to hold their clothes in place so they could fight without any encumbrances but even more importantly to hold the sheath that would contain the sword. The bible says to gird your loins with the belt of truth. Why? Because truth maintains the stability of the person wearing it. Without it, they can go off into many deceptions or vain imaginations. What I have seen in many Christians is that they may have the Sword of the Spirit, but they are not wearing their belt of Truth.

So having the Sword of the Spirit without Truth will inevitably lead to people being seduced or deceived. The Truth is the Word. We must be very careful to always speak the Truth, not what we think or our opinions which often come because people are not wearing a belt of truth. I have heard people say, "The Spirit of the Lord says," and you know full well after hearing it that was not from God. Unless you are wearing the Belt of Truth, you will not discern that.

The enemy loves it when you forget your belt because he is a master at imitating the Spirit which then leads into all kinds of wrong doctrine. For example, this is one of the most common of lies, "There are many ways to God and heaven; it doesn't matter how you get there" or "I live a good life, I feed the poor and give housing to those who need it. I do my share of good deeds." Some who call themselves Prophetesses and Prophets who are evil in disguise pander to those who are weak and need a word from God. So they will be happy to give you one for a price. I have seen people who are wielding the sword wildly, caught up in earthly things which have no business being in the house of God. You cannot mix the World with God's Word. It is what the apostate church is doing. It is unacceptable to God and it's like oil and vinegar—they don't mix.

I have heard people who have been Christians for years make statements like, "The philosophers have so much to offer and use their ideas to interject their thoughts into the Word." Paul tried that in Athens and found out that it didn't work (Acts 17). Later he realizes how wrong that is and goes back to the straight up gospel. You must only speak the Truth from the Word. Or they use psychology on people who need deliverance by putting a chair in the middle of a room and telling the person to talk to it as if their dead parent were present. Really???? Now this is so wrong on so many levels, but let us look at the severity of what they are doing. They are conjuring spirits and think this is perfectly okay. NO, it is not.

The world doesn't have the mind of Christ. Jesus never said, "Let's send so and so to the psychologist to get delivered." No, he stood before them and spoke the word with authority, and they were healed not just a bit but completely. Why is it we cannot believe for that today? Why is it that people think we need to add programs and psychology to the Word of God as if to say that was good then, but now we are so much more complicated and need outside intervention. Really??? Do you really think human beings have changed that much?

Jesus didn't tell the young man he delivered from a legion of demons, "Okay, now that you are delivered, you might want to go see a psychologist to help you overcome all the stuff from your past." **<u>NO, HE DIDN"T because when Jesus sets you free, you are free indeed.</u>** Why then does the church continually fall into the trap of Satan and think we need to do these things? Because people want an easy fix. We live in a microwave society—if I can't have it right away, I will walk away. Has it occurred to anyone that maybe God wants them to feel the pain that He wants to deliver them from? Perhaps God has a plan different than what you think? Can you believe for a miracle even if it is not immediate?

Now I am not saying we can't talk about our experiences so we can see how the enemy has played us, but the world's system isn't going to deliver you. There are certain situations where a person may have to have vigilant care. Such as those who are battling suicide for instance and do not receive their deliverance immediately. I believe God will deliver them, but we don't know how or what took them to the state of mind they are in and we cannot be there 24 hours a day to watch over them. So in a case like that, I think it is wise to call in reinforcements like a clinic who can keep watch over them. But we continue to pray until we see the deliverance manifest. Sometimes it is medications creating the problem. In some cases, it's sin preventing their deliverance. In any case, there are times to use wisdom and ask for assistance.

I recall standing for years for a mate. Many told me to stop being so picky and just date, but that was not what God wanted for me, and I am so happy I listened to the Lord. Today, 20 years later, I am married to a wonderful, faithful man of God who I cherish. Had I listened to the world, I would probably be in a mess today. Why am I bringing this up? Mainly because we have watered down the gospel to be ineffectual and incorporated the worlds system and believe that this will bring a better result. It is a lie from the pit of hell. How do you overcome these deceptions? By wearing the Belt of Truth—the Word of God. It exposes every wile of the enemy no matter the subject or situation. The problem is that people don't read the Word except on Sunday or read some simple devotion daily thinking that will get them through. The Word of God says," *Study to shew thyself approved unto God, a workman that needeth not to be ashamed, **<u>rightly dividing the word of TRUTH</u>**" (2 Timothy 2:15).*

So what does this boil down to? Without the BELT OF TRUTH, the SWORD OF THE SPIRIT can be lost. So wear your belt and sheath your sword and when you need the cutting edge of the blade of the Spirit, it will be unsheathed from Truth, the Word of God, and not of yourself.

BREASTPLATE

The next piece of armor is the **BREASTPLATE OF RIGHTEOUSNESS**. The breastplate was most commonly made of metal and sometimes leather pieces attached for comfort. As I tried to picture the Roman soldiers wearing these metal breastplates, it is obvious what their function was—to protect the heart and all the important internal organs of life. For if any vital organ was struck, it would be immediate death. Now if they wore this on the battle field, this would be pretty uncomfortable if it was scorching heat or freezing cold, so wouldn't that have burned their skin or caused frostbite? The answer is yes, but they didn't wear it against their skin. They wore a heavy cloth garment underneath it to prevent that from happening.

Spiritually, I could see all kinds of revelation here—starting with the robe worn underneath the shield. I recalled Aaron being told to wear the garment of the priest and the breastplate of the 12 stones representing Israel over the priestly garment close to his heart.

*"Have Aaron your brother brought to you from among the Israelites, along with his sons Nadab and Abihu, Eleazar and Ithamar, so they may serve me as priests. 2 Make sacred garments for your brother Aaron to give him dignity and honor. 3 Tell all the skilled workers to whom I have given wisdom in such matters that they are to make garments for Aaron, for his **consecration**, so he may **serve me as priest**. 4 These are the*

garments they are to make: a breast piece, an ephod, a robe, a woven tunic, a turban and a sash. They are to make these sacred garments for your brother Aaron and his sons, so they may serve me as priests. 5 Have them use gold, and blue, purple and scarlet yarn, and fine linen." Exodus 28:1-5

Exodus 28:29 29: "And Aaron shall bear the names of the children of Israel in the breastplate of judgment upon his heart, when he goeth in unto the holy place, for a memorial before the Lord continually."

What we see here is a multitude of revelation for the armor talked about in the new testament.

First, God says they are sacred garments. This means not everyone can wear them. It indicates that only those who are called by His name may wear it designating that the person has been given a position of honor and dignity. What does that mean to us? That the armor of the Lord is sacred and when worn indicates the person has been assigned dignity and honor by God. So can a sinner wear this garment?

NO. Can a person who thinks there is a great creator but doesn't believe that Yeshua/Jesus is Lord wear it? NO. Only the blood bought church, the redeemed who have been consecrated to the Lord, can wear this garment for it is holy unto the Lord, given as protection against the enemy. Notice the Robe and Tunic worn by the priest this is the righteousness of Yeshua Messiah.

Job 29:14: "I put on righteousness, and it clothed me: my judgment was as a robe and a diadem."

Isaiah 61:10: "I will greatly rejoice in the LORD, my soul shall be joyful in my God; for he hath clothed me with the garments of salvation, he hath covered me with the robe of righteousness, as a bridegroom decketh himself with ornaments, and as a bride adorneth herself with her jewels."

So as we put the Robe and Breastplate of Righteousness over our hearts, we are protected because He is our righteousness. The Word of God says in *Isaiah 54:17 (New King James Version (NKJV)):*

*"No weapon formed against you shall prosper,
And every tongue which rises against you in judgment
You shall condemn.
This is the heritage of the servants of the Lord,
And their righteousness is from Me,"
Says the Lord."*

"Then your light will break forth like the dawn, and your healing will quickly appear; then your righteousness will go before you, and the glory of the LORD will be your rear guard" (NIV Isaiah 58:8).

First, I want you all to notice that in Isaiah 61 he compares the garments of salvation to a bride and bridegroom decked out and adorned. Not anybody, the bride and groom are special and are adorned with jewels. In other words, they are made more beautiful by God's hand in delivering the garments of salvation.

Now notice that Breastplates only covered the front of a person. Your back would always be exposed to the enemy, but the Word of God says He is our rear guard. If He is my rear guard, then I never have to sound retreat, give up, or surrender to the enemy or ever be in fear. So why is it that when many Christians face an obstacle, trial, or temptation, their first reaction is fear and running away? Others choose to remove their breastplate so they can be more comfortable in the world. Do you not believe God will be your rear guard? I don't know about you, but I wouldn't want anyone else as my rear guard but the Lord. I know He will never leave me nor forsake me; that is His promise. I know we are human and there are times we face great obstacles, but it is time we stand firm and advance, letting the enemy know we have the greater power within us. Victory is ours.

Wearing your Robe and Breastplate of Righteousness tells the enemy we belong to the King of Kings and Lord of Lords and His

Righteousness covers our sins for they are completely forgiven and forgotten. Buried in the deepest sea, no longer can your past haunt you. Don't let people dredge that old man up either, because I tell you the truth—they will try. I recently had that experience. So glad I had my armor on.

This person was very close to me and knew every mistake or sin I had ever committed in the past and wanted to dredge that old man up because he was apparently convicted by the change in me. I wasn't that person anymore, and in fact that person no longer existed. I am being very straight with you right now; there will be people who will try to knock you down with your past. Don't you let them. Even Christians might be at fault here. It is usually one thing or another, either jealousy of what God has been doing in you or conviction, so they want to feel better about their own life choices that are sinful.

I can tell you that the day that happened, immediately God spoke to me and said, "You don't have to listen to that. I forgave all that long ago and don't remember it, and I don't want you to remember it either." I stood up and boldly repeated what God said to me and then I said, "I feel sorry for you because if that is all you can say, we have nothing more to talk about. I will not engage in this conversation, but I think you should be ashamed of yourself for attempting to defame me in front of others." I assure you that sent a shock wave through the room.

I left immediately thereafter. You see, the enemy can use anyone to drag you back to the position of guilt and hate of oneself. But if you are wearing your breastplate, you realize that the blood of Yeshua has cleansed and given you a new life and all you see is His righteousness, oh Hallelujah. Don't ever let the enemy rob you of what God has already done for you. He has a loud roar but no teeth. He sounds scary but, in fact, has no power over you because of the Breastplate of Righteousness. I will say this, too—the same people who try to attack you will soon see you are a warrior of the Lord and will back off because Satan is a coward and knows what power you possess in the Holy Ghost.

FEET SHOD WITH THE PREPARATION OF PEACE

For years, I wondered what having your feet shod might mean other than the obvious. Then one day, God revealed to me in a very simplistic way that even I could understand, "DUH....Battle imagine fighting a battle without shoes?" I responded with "Aha."

The Roman Army wore shoes that protected the front top of their feet and laced up the calf to ensure that they were securely fastened and protecting the Achilles tendon which prevented the enemy from paralyzing you. They had metal nails or tacks of sorts on the bottom which we get the word "cleat" from, which means to supply, support, give traction, and strengthen the wearer. With cleats, one can run faster because the cleats dig into the earth and propel the person forward while maintaining stabilization regardless of terrain.

Can you imagine going into battle with flip flops? First of all, you would not have stability, and your speed of movement would be greatly diminished. Recently, I saw an episode of the Island where the person was walking on the jagged beach rocks with flip flops on. Initially, he was careful and the rocks were dry and moving about was tedious but possible. Then the tide started rolling in, and as he stepped out, he began to slip and slide, eventually falling onto the jagged rocks. It appeared that the person had hurt his back and could not move. He was done and the game over for him.

I sat and contemplated how that happens to us when we don't wear the shoes of the Preparation of Peace. God may take you over your emotional, financial, or personal terrain. Your feet will not have sure footing or grip properly if you don't have the shoes laced and securely fastened ready to go knowing full well we are God's and He is our God. Stand still and say, "If God be for me, who can be against me. Amen?" This is our stability that we have peace with God. I see this often not only in others but in my own home. Attack comes and first response is I am reeling, and why? Because I am not wearing my shoes. If we have our peace on, nothing can move us, not even the slippery, jagged rocks of Satan's attacks. Our shoes of the preparation of peace give us stability as they grip into the peace and knowledge of the Lord.

Romans 10:14-15 NIV:
"How, then, can they call on the one they have not believed in? And how can they believe in the one of whom they have not heard? And how can they hear without someone preaching to them? 15 And how can anyone preach unless they are sent? As it is written: "How beautiful are the feet of those who bring good news!""

Why are these feet beautiful? Because they bring PEACE, SHALOM PEACE.

John 14:27 NIV:
"Peace I leave with you; my peace I give you. I do not give to you as the world gives. Do not let your hearts be troubled and do not be afraid."

Luke 10:19-20:
"Behold, I give unto you power to tread on serpents and scorpions, and over all the power of the enemy: and nothing shall by any means hurt you. Notwithstanding in this rejoice not, that the spirits are subject unto you; but rather rejoice, because your names are written in heaven."

Peace, Shalom Peace, the peace that surpasses all understanding. That peace comes from knowing God and sharing the Gospel. We often look around and see so many perishing from the battle. I often ask myself, "Why are they suffering so much? Are they not wearing their shoes of the Preparation of Peace?" What I learned is that so often people are not wearing their shoes or, worse, they have them on but never lace them up. Their thoughts are always negative. They can't seem to find any faith within. Now don't get me wrong folks, sometimes we all experience a bit of the self pity, but when we do, we should immediately address ourselves and refocus. Lace up your shoes.

Look, if our feet are shod with the preparation of peace, then when trouble comes, we don't fall apart; we encourage ourselves in the Lord. Why? Because we are His, and we have been delivering the Gospel to others, but as we do, we reinforce our own walk. People are out there stumbling over their peace because they haven't laced up their shoes. What happens when you don't lace your shoes? Eventually you will topple over, stumble, and fall. What do you think is happening in the church today? Yes, that is right; people are falling, primarily due to their own decisions either not to wear the shoes or to wear them improperly. Or worse, someone has encouraged them to try these more comfortable worldly shoes that they claim work just as good. NOT.

You must lace up those shoes, protect the Word that is in you so when the trouble comes, you speak to the trouble from the Word of God and it must bow to the Word. Your shoes determine your stability, and you stand rock solid, immoveable. Correct bad standing by correcting what you are standing on. Is it the Word or your thoughts? This improves your walk because now you can run with assurance and be protected from invading enemies and evil spirits. You see, when your posture in Christ starts to slump, I have to ask you, are you wearing your shoes?

When you come in to worship the Lord on Sunday morning and you are dragging in like the whole world is on your shoulders, I have to ask, are you wearing your shoes? When you say, "I am struggling with this sin in my life; I can't seem to overcome," I have to ask, are you wearing your shoes? When you are tossed to and fro in your faith hot one minute and cold the next minute, you are lost, I have to ask, are you wearing your shoes."But Ms. Scotti, you don't know what I have been through." No, I don't, but God does. And the Word says He has given us power over ALL the power of the enemy. Over how much of the enemy? **<u>ALL the power of the enemy.</u>**

All that means is there is nothing that can stand in your way of worship or speaking the gospel. Rejoice because you already have the victory, you are merely waiting for the manifestation of the victory. Don't be afraid when the world treats you unjustly, but rather speak the Word into the situation. Trust me, God will avenge you and restore you. Why do I know this? Because He has done it for me and God is not a respecter of persons. You too can be avenged and restored.

Recently, I was unjustly released from my position as a hygienist. It was an evil act that was perpetrated against me. Lies and defamation were swirling about me. My first reaction was human; I was hurt, especially since I had worked for the man for nearly 5 years. But within a few minutes, the Word of the Lord came through my mouth and out into the atmosphere."I am a child of the King. I need not fear for He will send an army out against my foe. He will avenge and He will restore and no weapon Satan can form against me will prosper for my God, the God of Israel, will never forsake me by the blood of the Lamb in Yeshua. That is where I put my trust and He alone is my advocate. Finally Lord, I pray blessings upon this man because your word says by doing so, I heap coals upon his head and perhaps he might be saved as his sin is revealed to him. I forgive without response not for his sake, but for my own sake, for no root of bitterness will I allow to take root in me for YOU and YOU alone do I serve."

Let me tell you, there was a major release in me. Sure, my feelings were hurt, but we don't go by our feelings. They will lead us down the wrong path. If I allowed my feelings to rule I might have gone after revenge. Don't let a root of bitterness put you on the wrong path. Our faith is in Yeshua knowing full well He will deliver us. What that person meant to harm me with God turned it totally around and brought me good. In so doing, I have perfect peace.

I have learned to wear my armor at all times. I never take it off because you know what? The enemy can attack you even while you sleep. I can tell you this because it has happened to me. I recently counseled a woman who had had similar experience. Look folks, as warriors, we are in this together, so don't neglect the assembly of believers because someone hurt your feelings. They are human, too, and we need each other to stand watch over each other. In the Marines when we were out on patrol, one person stayed awake for a period of time to watch and guard over the others. Every four hour, that one person would be replaced so there were always fresh eyes watching out for the troops. So it is with us. We stand watch over the weak and newly saved and those who are sick through prayer. Do not neglect your prayer time, especially if God calls you to pray for someone it may be that you are the fresh eyes praying over that person or situation. Do not neglect your scheduled watch whatever time of day that is.

SHIELD OF FAITH

Have you been under attack? Have the arrows of the enemy been striking you, true and fast? Are you trying to fight but you have been so mortally wounded that you feel like giving up? My question to you is where is your Shield of Faith? I sometimes wonder if people left their shield hanging up. Others are carrying it but not properly, and still others say they don't have any faith left. Really????? But the Word of God says, *"For by the grace given me I say to every one of you: Do not think of yourself more highly than you ought, but rather think of yourself with sober judgment, in accordance* **with the faith God has distributed to each of you"** *(Romans 12:3).*

Could it be that you feel you should have been delivered already? After all, Joe Smoe got delivered in a day; why can't I? Perhaps his faith was greater than yours, my friend, or maybe God is trying to increase your faith through the trial. Or maybe there is something God wants you to lay down. Or maybe God is preparing something special just for you. Did you ever think of that! No, of course not, because you live in a society that expects everything to be immediate satisfaction. In fact, this is the hardest thing for millennials and younger generations, because they have grown up in the computer age and everything is at their fingertips and moves at the speed of light. They expect God to be the same. Sorry, but God doesn't work that way. You would always remain a baby if he just kept you on milk. Paul said in *Hebrews 5:13, "Anyone who lives on milk, being still an infant, is not acquainted with the teaching about righteousness."*

So in order for your faith to grow and for you to mature in the faith, you must be acquainted with righteousness, and how is that done, you ask? Through the Word and the Holy Spirit. As you go through the trials, your faith increases and solid food can now be administered. During that trial, elders may guide you and correct you. Don't take offense, but be willing to be corrected as in the correction faith again grows. Soon you will develop into a mature follower of Yeshua. So if you leave faith home or just drag your faith shield around, you will never be protected. Because it only functions as a protection when it is in use. Hold it firmly before you. Do not set it down for anything, even when you are tired. Hide behind it that the arrows of the enemy may not penetrate.

My husband did a sermon on the shield I thought was so good. I share it here for the purpose of encouragement and instruction.

Roman soldiers were given a shield called a Scutum. It could be as tall as three feet tall and was rectangular. This shield had more than one purpose. First, if held by the handle in the middle of the inside of the shield, which by the way was called the boss (I found that an interesting factoid), they could cover their entire bodies just about. If they stood shoulder to shoulder in a square, they not only covered themselves but protected their comrades from being attacked from behind. Also, the shield had a layer of leather which was soaked in water till saturated. After it was fully saturated, it would then be rubbed with olive oil so that when those fiery darts or arrows hit the shield, they would be fully extinguished.

What are the fiery darts to us today? Is it your finances, a love lost, worldly gain, sickness? Think about that. Know your weaknesses; those are what Satan will attack you with. He will send fiery darts of doubt, dissatisfaction, and deceit to stop your testimony of the Gospel. When we hold the shield of faith and open ourselves to the Word, we allow the Holy Spirit to saturate us and anoint us with oil for service.

Finally, it was said that this shield was so large and heavy that it could actually knock over an opponent, thereby making him susceptible to the sword and ultimately death. The Roman army would stand shoulder to shoulder in unity shields up and over their head, creating like a shell and advancing. Can you picture this? Huge Roman army marching towards the enemy, full shield up, arrows bouncing off their shields, fire bouncing off their shields, swords having no ability to penetrate, and suddenly, the enemy is underfoot as they fell over. The next row would kill them off, leaving a trail of dead bodies. Oh, yeah, that excites me because when we fight in unity not thinking one is better than another, we advance. We will leave a trail of dead demons and circumstances on the battle field. When we look back, we will see the enemy has been defeated. Oh, Glory to God. What power God has given us. Remember, though, unity is the key here.

Now I have a question. Do you think at any time they put their shields down? If they did, someone else had taken the watch with their shield at the ready—another reason why we need each other. Sometimes, the battle is hot and very hard and we are tired. We need each other to hold us up during those times. Imagine trying to fight a battle without a shield like that. Or perhaps a shield the size of a your hand. How much protection would that be? So although God gives each of us a measure of faith, He also causes the increase through the Holy Spirit bringing you through the trials and testing.

Your shield is the first thing that the enemy sees and knows it will protect you. The Word says it protects you from all the fiery darts. It is your first defensive instrument. That is why we are told not to get tired in well doing. We must hold up that shield of faith.

When we doubt or fear or worry, it's like Peter walking on the water or like Elijah hiding in the cave—we take our eyes off God and look at our circumstances. When we do that, bam, the enemy is right there to kill you off. He can only get to you if you lower your shield. Stay strong, don't give up, encourage yourself in the Lord and in the Word of his promises.

Some people have told me that they feel like they are in the fire. Well, I believe that can happen when the enemy is shooting fiery darts and your shield isn't well oiled or saturated with water. What, you say? The water is a representation of the Holy Spirit and the Oil is the anointing. How do you get those two things to drench you? The only way is in the Word, praising, and in our prayer closets or War Rooms. If you haven't seen the movie War Room, you should. It will encourage you to find a quiet place in your home where you can commune with God in prayer and the Word—seeking after God, spending time in the Word, and allowing Him to pour out His anointing on you. Without it, you will not survive.

James said something that I always wondered about. He said, "Faith without works is dead." What I think he was saying there is, not that works make faith grow, but rather that faith is our hope in our hearts, but it must be put into action and action is works. Faith is a thought, a hope, a belief. It becomes a hand grenade when we put faith into action, blowing the enemy right out of sight. Now if you can visualize this, that is what a full on attack looks like. It's advancing on the enemy without any thought of retreat. The next time you are attacked with an arrow from the enemy, make sure your shield is anointed with oil and saturated with the Holy Ghost. Then you can hold up your shield and advance boldly for as you do, you will overtake and overcome and be victorious and the enemy will flee.

HELMET OF SALVATION

This is one of my favorite pieces of armor because I see this piece as covered in the blood. When I put it on, I am covered in the blood of Yeshua, and the enemy cannot beat me up with my past.

Psalm 27:1:
"The Lord is my Light and my Salvation, whom shall I fear?"

2 Corinthians 10:3-5:
"Indeed, we live as human beings, but we do not wage war according to human standards; for the weapons of our warfare are not merely human, but they have divine power to destroy strongholds. We destroy arguments and every proud obstacle raised up against the knowledge of God, and we take every thought captive to obey Christ."

If the Word of God tells us we have divine power to destroy strongholds, arguments, and every proud obstacle raised up against the knowledge of God and that we can take captive every thought to obey Christ, why are so many Christians falling away from the faith, dying on the battle field, overcome by stress, fear, and sorrow, feeling hopeless in the battle? The answer is simple—they are either not wearing their helmet or perhaps not wearing it properly.

Let's talk about what the Helmet of Salvation is and what and how it protects. First, it protects our minds. Where does the enemy attack us primarily? In the mind. I want to stop and dwell here for a moment because it is so important to understand that when we are saved, born again, and filled with the Holy Ghost, we are given the mind of Christ.

1 Corinthians 2:16 – "For who hath known the mind of the Lord, that he may instruct him? But we have the mind of Christ."

Romans 12:2 – "And be not conformed to this world: but be ye transformed by the renewing of your mind, that ye may prove what [is] that good, and acceptable, and perfect, will of God."

If then we have been given the mind of Christ, what shall we fear? Nothing, for He is our salvation no matter what we come up against in life. I believe people who are affected by life's circumstances are often not wearing or just carrying their helmets. This leaves their minds open to attack and let's face it, folks, this is the main battlefield. Also, how can your mind be renewed if you are not wearing your helmet?

Imagine for a moment a Roman soldier without a helmet. As they advance, where do you suppose the enemy is going to try and strike? His head, that is right. But why? Because the enemy knows if he can strike the head, the soldier will immediately die and no longer be a threat. It stops the soldier dead in his tracks, literally. Today, if you are in the military or have been in the military, what is one of the most important pieces of gear? Your helmet, that is right!

Spiritually, Satan has the same plan. You see, he knows you are a child of God and he hates God, so he hates you, too. His whole purpose is to destroy the children of God before they destroy his kingdom by their testimony. He knows if he can attack your mind he can keep you bound up forever at minimum and at the most, totally kill you off. We can see this in suicide victims. You are bound up if you are fretting all the time. You are killed off when you give up and say God isn't going to help me so I gotta help myself.

First of all, get your doggone helmet on, now speak the word to that situation. God isn't giving up on you. He may delay, but He is never late. The trial is working patience in you. Don't try to outthink God; you can't .His ways are not your ways, but if you stand wearing your helmet of salvation reminding Satan that you are a child of God and the King of Kings and Lord of Lords is your master and only to him will I bow, you are reminding Satan that you are a blood bought child of God. He has no power over you, and now you can pull out your sword with faith and believe for victory. Cut that demon of depression down, strike the fatal blow to adultery, and pornography.

Wield that sword against anger and hate, cutting it out to the root. You can then look back and see the many victories God has given you because you were obedient and wore your helmet of Salvation which kept your mind on Him and not the lies perpetrated by the enemy.

I have heard people say, "Well, you just don't understand what a struggle I am in. The devil is really beating me up." Really??? Where is your helmet? Are you wearing it or what? "I can't break free of this addiction or sin." Really? Then you must not be wearing your helmet of salvation. In fact, do you have one? Let me tell you, folks, just because you go to church or are a good person doesn't mean you get the armor. Some of you said the salvation prayer, but it stopped there. You didn't turn from your sin. You went right back to it like a dog to his vomit as the bible says. Then you come to church and delve out a series of excuses why you are still in the sin. I propose to you that you may need to go back to the altar and repent. For some, saying the prayer was just that you said it and now it's done. But the word of God says in *Ez.18:30*, *"Therefore, O house of Israel, I will judge you, each one according to his ways, declares the Sovereign LORD. Repent!* **Turn away** *from all your offenses; then sin will not be your downfall" (NIV).*

> *Acts 3:19 (NIV): "Repent, then, and turn to God, so that your sins may be wiped out, that times of refreshing may come from the Lord."*

Now please don't get me wrong; we will all sin at some time or another during our walk with God, but if we are seeking the Lord and reading His Word, it will expose those areas that need to be changed. It will prick your heart to repentance. The bible says we will not achieve perfection until we are called home, but Paul said to strive towards the mark of the high calling of God.

Philipians 3:14:
"I press toward the mark for the prize of the high calling of God in Christ Jesus."

But as believers, we are to be ever pressing onward to the calling of the Master. So when we are on the verge of sin, the Holy Spirit is faithful to prick our hearts to stop us and not go in that direction. If we are walking in the Spirit daily, we will hear that arrest and stop, turn around, and go in the opposite direction. This is why it is so important to remain filled with the Holy Spirit.

We will talk further on this infilling later, but for now, lets' focus on wearing the helmet.

In addition to protecting your mind, the helmet of salvation protects your ears from hearing what is not good or Godly. Your eyes are shielded from the attacks of the enemy that would tempt your eyes to see what is ungodly and an abomination to the Lord. Finally, it protects your mouth. I can tell you from my own experience when I fell into sin, it was because I took off my helmet and my mind was deceived into believing it was okay and boom, I fell. I would get up only because of the grace of God and repent and put the helmet back on. But how often have we all done this. The mouth can be the major pitfall to an individual as this is what the Word of God says *in Luke 6:45: "A good person produces good things from the treasury of a good heart, and an evil person produces evil things from the treasury of an evil heart.* What you say flows from what is in your heart."

> *Psalm 37:30, 31:*
> "*The mouths of the righteous utter wisdom, and their tongues speak what is just. The law of his God is in his heart; his feet do not slip.*"

> *Proverbs 10:11:*
> "*The mouth of the righteous is a fountain of life, but the mouth of the wicked conceals violence.*"

There are ever so many scriptures about the mouth as it can be a weapon of destruction or building up. Proverbs is one of my favorite books, and I read a chapter every day with a chapter from another book. Why? Because there is so much wisdom and teaching of how we should walk in faith.

What you speak into the atmosphere is going to be positive or negative; it's up to you. I once heard a scientist say that every spoken word we have ever said is still traveling through the universe—it never ends. I don't know about you, but that is truly something that causes me to rein in my thoughts and heart to speak only what is good and lovely. Do I miss it sometimes? Yes, and I repent when I do. Think about this for a moment—if it is true our words never end, then when the day of judgment comes, I believe God will be able to play back all we did and said. I will bet you are all thinking, "Oh my goodness, I am in deep doo doo. I lost my temper with my husband or wife and said some really horrible, sinful things." Well, there is good news. When we repent and ask God to forgive our mistakes, he wipes them clean like using whiteout. However, does that mean you can just keep on doing it and asking God to forgive you over and over again for the same sin? Paul said I think not, for we then make the blood of no avail.

Heb 10:26-27 "If we deliberately keep on sinning after we have received the knowledge of the truth, no sacrifice for sins is left, but only a fearful expectation of judgment and of raging fire that will consume the enemies of God." NIV

This is how John says we will know we are in Christ: 1 John 2:5-6, "This is how we know we are in him: Whoever claims to live in him must walk as Jesus did." NIV

So what am I getting at here? I am saying keep your eyes, ears, and mouth protected with the helmet of salvation for the enemy wants to distract you and destroy your testimony. How? By getting you to remove it so you expose your eyes and ears to the sins of the world enticing you away from God and even worse, to find fault and get you to speak against God. He tried this with Job. Do you remember his wife told him, "Why don't you curse God and die?" This is how the enemy will work if you take off your helmet.

Now I am going to share something about wearing your helmet at all times. Before I go to bed at night, I pray and thank God for my salvation. I thank Him for my deliverance and for the protection I have under the blood afforded me through my helmet of Salvation. Do you know why I do this? Because the enemy does not sleep ever. He is constantly trying to kill off people, even in the dark of night. He will enter your dreams, disrupt your sleep with thoughts of fear and anxiety. You will even think of how much fun (his thoughts of fun) you used to have while you were sinning. He will talk to you in your sleep. "Did you see that drop dead gorgeous hottie at the coffee shop? Bet you could have her. Wouldn't that be fun? Or did you see that guy? He is looking at you. He wants you bad, and he's loaded. He could show you a really good time, and you would never want for anything again. That little drink of Jack Daniels won't hurt you. Look, they even found some benefits to having some. Don't believe that junk that you are an alcoholic. Just one doesn't make you an alcoholic. Hey, remember that site on the computer that showed some hot pornography? It's still there. No one will know, and you can sneak away to watch it now. Your wife is fast asleep. Come on now, you are entitled to a little entertainment." These are just a few of the attacks that can come in the night. Don't be caught off guard and without your helmet. Wearing your helmet will save you from all the deceptions of the enemy.

Now that you understand the armor, put it all on, keep it on, be vigilant because the Word of God says that the enemy goes to and fro looking for whom he may devour.

I like the way the People's Bible says it in 1 Peter 5:8: "Be sober. Sobriety is necessary to vigilance. Be vigilant. Wide awake and watchful. The reason follows. An enemy is ready to spring upon them. The devil, as a roaring lion, walketh about, seeking whom he may devour. He goeth about as the lion, seeking for prey. The lion while hunting only roars when it springs. So the devil is stealthy and does not give warning of his approach."

Check it out. The devil isn't going to announce he is going to attack. He is stealthy, never giving a warning, because his whole purpose is to catch you off guard without your armor on. He is looking for the weak, the foolish, the lazy, and the sneaky. Now you know who you are. We were all once in these categories, but praise God we have been delivered and made wise by the Word, so we must wear our armor all the time.

Many years ago, when I was a baby Christian, I wasn't always preparing my mind for the attack. I wasn't always wearing my armor. One night in the middle of the night, I had the sickest dream. It woke me from a dead sleep. I realized immediately the enemy was attacking me in my sleep because I wasn't covered in my armor. I prayed and asked the Lord to remove this buffeting of the enemy, and God did. I got out of bed, read the bible for about 20 minutes, and went back to sleep without a recurrence. I learned something that night. I never go to bed without prayer and reading the Word of God, even if it is just a verse only. I can tell you that never happened again, and I continue to pray and read each night and each morning.

You can be prey if you are not covering your mind with your helmet and armor. Nowadays, the attacks have become far more aggressive as I hear story after story about people being attacked in their sleep. Be vigilant, my friends. Keep that armor on at all times.

Chapter 4

THE GATES

When I was a little girl going to children's church, I remember singing this song called, "Be careful, little eyes." When I was a child, I really didn't understand the full impact of that song, and, frankly, I think this song should be sung by all of us daily. I really was quickened to share this song with you as it is a very strong teaching tool.

> O, be careful little eyes what you see,
> O, be careful little eyes what you see.
> For the Father up above
> He's looking down in love,
> So, be careful, little eyes, what you see.

And continued.......

O, be careful little ears, what you hear
O, be careful little ears, what you hear

O, be careful, little tongue, what you say
O, be careful, little tongue, what you say

O, be careful, little hands, what you do
O, be careful, little hands, what you do

O, be careful, little feet, where you go
O, be careful, little feet, where you go

O, be careful, little heart, whom you trust
O, be careful, little heart, whom you trust
For the Father up above
He's looking down in love
So, be careful, little heart, whom you trust.

Be careful little eyes.

I am reminded of how many times I had to cover my eyes when watching a movie that had scary scenes. My spirit could never handle it. I wondered why everyone else didn't appear to be moved by it, but I was horrified. In fact, if I did I watch them I often would have nightmares. I realized early on my spirit was sensitive to those types of movies and never went to one again. What others found funny and scary but enjoyable, I found horrifying. I learned just because someone else isn't affected by something doesn't mean you shouldn't be too.

The eyes are major gates to the soul. It is here Satan tempted Jesus with, "Look what I can give you." He tempted His eyes with the pleasures and grandeur of having it all.

Strangely enough, Satan hasn't changed, but now he has become more aggressive. Today, our young men and women are exposed to horrifying sexual acts on video and the internet, which are truly abominations before the Lord. Pornography was always looked down upon in the past, but today Satan's followers make it look like it's normal and okay, because it's entertainment. We can take this a step further with all the vampire movies and witchcraft, murder, and suicide—all demonic in nature.

Different forms of sexuality (whether homosexual, bisexual, or transsexual) are now taught in the schools as normal people can't help themselves. Now we have a new one attacking our kids: Islam. Teachers have given kids assignments to desensitize them to the Muslim religion. A sixth grader was forced to wear a hijab as an act of understanding the religion. People of God, if this is happening in your school, you need to yank your kids out of the public school system to send a message.

There was a time when you would never see a sexual scene or hear a swear word on TV. What has happened to our leaders? Have they lost their sense of morality? Turn the TV off if necessary. My husband and I watch mostly house renovations, cooking shows, and game shows, but occasionally we look for a wholesome movie. However, those are few and far between in today's movies.

Next, be careful little ears what you hear. Be careful little tongue what you say.

I recently saw a video that was supposed to be funny, but it was not. I was stunned. When a five year old is put on YouTube spouting every evil word that could be said and the parents are in the background laughing because they think it's so cute, beware: this will be the same child who swears at a police officer or tells the teacher off.

We have been watching these events unfolding in Baltimore and other locations. Don't be blind open your eyes Dr Spock wasn't right, spanking won't kill the child trust me I had a few beatings in my childhood and it taught me one thing…..respect. Obedience was the second thing. I see children beating on the parent in the market and I just want to go over and shake the parent and say discipline the child for Pete's sake. But today we can't do that because some CPS officer may show up at your door and say you are abusive. My God help us to be brave enough to discipline and teach our children good morals.

I mention Baltimore a moment ago, here again.

Be careful little hands and feet what you do and where you go.

Folks used the Baltimore incident to riot and to loot a store, totally stealing every expensive item they could get their hands on. Satan has found how to reach the youth: *greed* and *money*, and things have become their objects of desire. They idolize people like Bruce Jenner who wants to be a woman. Where is the outcry of Christianity? Why aren't we talking about this man's poor decision which is entirely selfish without any regard for his children's feelings? The attitude is, "I was always like this." NO, you weren't. You choose to be like this. He thinks this will change his life, but once changed, he will find himself just as empty as he was as Bruce. Because the only thing that will fill that empty place is the God of Israel.

We need to pray for the men and women in our society that are succumbing to the wiles of the enemy to say they are just as normal as you and I if they choose to be homosexual or transsexual. This is the way Sodom and Gommorah were before they were destroyed. People want to make Christians out to be haters. We don't hate the person, but we hate what is happening to those people because we know that from the beginning of time, Satan has a main purpose— the fall of man away from God. People of God, don't allow yourselves to be desensitized by what you see and say, "Well, that is their life. As long as it doesn't interfere with mine, I am okay with it."

No, no, no. That is how we got into this mess to begin with. Too many of us sat back and said those very words. I will admit, I am just as guilty. But God expects us to stand for the Word and not conform to this world. We hate the sin, but we love the sinner because we know God loves him or her, too. The word of God says that the Father sent his son for us all and that ALL might be saved.

Finally, be careful little heart whom you trust.

My older brother always told me that I was naïve. I still am to some degree, but I am better than I once was. I trusted everyone. I thought it was right to trust someone until they showed they couldn't be trusted. What I learned was what my brother taught me was true—a person must earn your trust. I began to see that the only person I could ever truly completely trust was the Lord. People will fail you—they are human and susceptible to the wiles of the enemy.

The bible says, *"Trust in the Lord with all thine heart and lean not to your own understanding....in all your ways submit to him and he will make your paths straight" (Proverbs 3:5-6).*

When we submit to the Lord all that we do, then He is faithful to direct our paths so we will not stumble. There was a time when I had to cut lose some friends. I loved them, but they were not on the same path as I was, and often I found myself drained, trying to help them. I had to cut some people loose from my life because their influence on me was not in line with the Word of God and the call that was on my life. Do you have friends or relatives who drain the life out of you? Do you listen to their stories of how they are living a life away from God and yet they refuse to turn to God for deliverance because changing themselves is just not what they want to do? Oh, be careful little heart whom you trust.

Deuteronomy 11:8-31:

"Observe therefore all the commands I am giving you today, so that you may have the strength to go in and take over the land that you are crossing the Jordan to possess, 9 and so that you may live long in the land the Lord swore to your ancestors to give to them and their descendants, a land flowing with milk and honey. 10 The land you are entering to take over is not like the land of Egypt, from which you have come, where you planted your seed and irrigated it by foot as in a vegetable garden. 11 But the land you are crossing the Jordan to take possession of is a land of mountains and valleys that drinks rain from heaven. 12 It is a land the Lord your God cares for; the eyes of the Lord your God are continually on it from the beginning of the year to its end. 13 So if you faithfully obey the commands I am giving you today—to love the Lord your God and to serve him with all your heart and with all your soul— 14 then I will send rain on your land in its season, both autumn and spring rains, so that you may gather in your grain, new wine and olive oil. 15 I will provide grass in the fields for your cattle, and you will eat and be satisfied.

16 Be careful, or you will be enticed to turn away and worship other gods and bow down to them. 17 Then the Lord's anger will burn against you, and he will shut up the heavens so that it will not rain and the ground will yield no produce, and you will soon perish from the good land the Lord is giving you. 18

Fix these words of mine in your hearts and minds; tie them as symbols on your hands and bind them on your foreheads. 19 Teach them to your children, talking about them when you sit at home and when you walk along the road, when you lie down and when you get up. 20 Write them on the doorframes of your houses and on your gates, 21 so that your days and the days of your children may be many in the land the Lord swore to give your ancestors, as many as the days that the heavens are above the earth.

"22 If you carefully observe all these commands I am giving you to follow—to love the Lord your God, to walk in obedience to him and to hold fast to him— 23 then the Lord will drive out all these nations before you, and you will dispossess nations larger and stronger than you. 24 Every place where you set your foot will be yours: Your territory will extend from the desert to Lebanon, and from the Euphrates River to the Mediterranean Sea. 25 No one will be able to stand against you. The Lord your God, as he promised you, will put the terror and fear of you on the whole land, wherever you go.

"26 See, I am setting before you today a blessing and a curse— 27 the blessing if you obey the commands of the Lord your God that I am giving you today; 28 the curse if you disobey the commands of the Lord your God and turn from the way that I command you today by following other gods, which you have not known. 29 When the Lord your God has brought you into the land you

are entering to possess, you are to proclaim on Mount Gerizim the blessings, and on Mount Ebal the curses. 30 As you know, these mountains are across the Jordan, westward, toward the setting sun, near the great trees of Moreh, in the territory of those Canaanites living in the Arabah in the vicinity of Gilgal. 31 You are about to cross the Jordan to enter and take possession of the land the Lord your God is giving you. When you have taken it over and are living there, 32 be sure that you obey all the decrees and laws I am setting before you today."

Now many leaders in Christianity might say, well that is Old Testament, the old dispensation, and we are no longer UNDER the law. This is true, *but that doesn't mean it's destroyed and no longer of any use..* God didn't put anything in the bible that would ever become outdated. The commands are not for His good but for our good. Should we not continue to observe them even though we fail? That is what the blood of Yeshua did for us. I have heard preachers teach that the Old Testament is the old dispensation and we are under the New dispensation. Let's talk about that.

Chapter 5

OLD VERSUS NEW DISPENSATION WHAT DOES THAT MEAN?

This is what Paul said in Ephesians.

*"Having made known unto us the mystery of his will, according to his good pleasure which he hath purposed in himself: that in the **DISPENSATION** of the **fullness** of times he might **gather together in one all things** in Christ, both which are in heaven, and which are on earth; even in him" (Ephesians 1:9-10).*

What does the word dispensation really mean?

Webster says,

1. Exemption from a rule or usual requirement:
   Synonyms: exemption · immunity · exception · exoneration · reprieve ·

2. A system of order, government, or organization of a nation, community, etc., especially as existing at a particular time: Synonyms: system · order · arrangement · organization

Easton Bible dictionary says,

Dispensation

(Gr. oikonomia, "management," "economy").

- The method or scheme according to which God carries out his purposes towards men is called a dispensation. There are three dispensations, the Patriarchal, the Mosaic or Jewish, and the Christian. These were the many stages in God's unfolding of his purpose of grace toward men. The word is not found with this meaning in Scripture.

In the patriarchal dispensation, salvation was of faith and the shedding of blood in circumcision, in the Mosaic dispensation, was the shedding of the blood of a lamb and a scapegoat sent into the wilderness. In Christ dispensation, it is Yeshua's blood period, giving us grace, mercy and redemption. But all address sin, faithfulness; all address we can only be saved by God's dispensation and that salvation is in the *blood*. In all three dispensations, it was the shedding of blood to cover sin. It was not the doing away of the Law or Feasts of the Lord. There are a few of you right now who have shut this book because, well, all your life you heard that we are no longer under the Law and that is true; it no longer rules us, but it is a continual reminder of how God wants us to live. When they asked Jesus which of the commandments was the greatest, what did He say?

Matthew 22:37-40:
"Jesus said unto him, Thou shalt love the Lord thy God with all thy heart, and with all thy soul, and with all thy mind.
38 This is the first and great commandment.
39 And the second is like unto it, Thou shalt love thy neighbor as thyself.
40 On these two commandments hang all the law and the prophets."

Now I ask you, does that sound like the Law has no place in the new dispensation?

Of course it is relevant and useful as a guide establishing boundaries from which we operate in this life. Now I say this—those two commands are all encompassing because if we Love the Lord as directed, how can one fall into sin so easily? I do not think it is possible. Why? Because the Holy Spirit is within us, guiding and exposing the sin.

Secondly, to love your neighbor as yourself, whoever hated themselves and wanted to punish oneself? Well, okay, I guess you could end up in self-flagellation, but most people don't. If we want the best for ourselves, should we not want the same for our neighbor? So jealousy, hatred, covetousness, how can those cohabit with love?

That's right, they can't. So what is my point? We are under one dispensation—all of the old combined with the all of the new to create the new man who is under grace covered in the blood of the Lamb Yeshua, filled with the Spirit and baptized by fire purified for service. He has grafted each one who believes on Him into the root of Israel to become one with Israel. Yes, you heard me right—we are grafted into Israel, not the other way around.

What that means is *"ALL Scripture is inspired by God and is useful to teach us what is true and to make us realize what is wrong in our lives. It corrects us when we are wrong and teaches us to do what is right" (2 Timothy 3:16 NLV).*

Then if all scripture is inspired by God, should we not take the old with the new for our benefit? Certainly that would make sense, wouldn't it? This is the reason I chose Deuteronomy 11. It tells us exactly what God expected of us even though He knew we couldn't live up to it completely. Thus, it is His plan for our Salvation then and now. For again the word says in Romans 3:23, "For all have sinned and fallen short of the Glory of God." He told the Israelites to observe all the commands so they would have strength. Are you feeling weak in body or mind? Seek the commands of the Lord and be strengthened and live a long, healthy life. So if you love the Lord your God with all your heart and soul, serve Him and FAITHFULLY obey His commands. Rains will come in its season and you may gather the grain, new wine, and oil grass will grow for your livestock and you will eat and be satisfied. Today, that could translate to I will pour out a blessing upon you and you will have sufficient funds to buy food and not be in want, you will have good jobs that pay well and sustain you and your family. You will be HEALTHY and satisfied.

Then he says, "Be careful or you will be enticed to turn away and worship other gods and bow down to them." Have you ever met someone whose life took a drastic turn for the better? I don't mean just a bit better but big time better, like they hit the lottery type better. What do you suppose happens to most people when they acquire great sums of money? They buy things, that is right—houses, cars, boats, and vacations, etc. Suddenly, they put God on the back burner. Where God was once first, he has been replaced with things or other people. I actually have seen this progression in others myself. Money changes people, and the enemy loves that. When money becomes your god or the person who gave you the money becomes your god, you begin to worship them instead of God. The worse part of that is that Satan can now control you because he will keep you focused on more money, more things, more status more, admiration, etc. It will never be enough, like the two leeches "Give, give…"

Money can and will lead to greed if your eyes are not on Yeshua, which will push you for acquiring more money, and it never ends. Or worse, it ends in Spiritual death because the things of God no longer take priority in your life but now take a back seat to almost every other thing in your life. Soon you will find yourself in the black hole of despair when Satan takes it all back and leaves you destitute with nothing. Think of the many men who jumped from building during the stock market crash. They were rich one minute and destitute and depressed the next. Now the King of sin steps in and hopelessness takes over and they jump. Why? Because without God, there is only a black hole of hopelessness.

When those we know are experiencing the high of money, we can remind them who should come first, that money is a tool not a god, and that only God can fill that empty place. Remind them that God always comes first. If they do not heed your words, it is on them. God will judge. We need only be messengers of hope.

Chapter 6

HOPELESSNESS AND DEPRESSION

*Ephesians 6:12 WNT (I liked this translation for this verse): "For ours is not a conflict with mere flesh and blood, but with the **despotisms**, the **empires**, the <u>forces that control and govern this dark world</u>—the **spiritual hosts** of evil arrayed against us in **the heavenly warfare**."*

What is a despot? Webster's dictionary says,

: A ruler who has total power and who often uses that power in cruel and unfair ways

: A person who has a lot of power over other people

Hello, that would be Satan and the forces and spiritual hosts are all the demons or fallen angels. He wants to kill you and the testimony of the Lord. He will not stop at anything to accomplish that goal. The bible says in 1 Peter 5:8, "Be sober, be vigilant; because your adversary the devil, as a roaring lion, walketh about, seeking whom he may devour." His intentions are to scare you to death or kill you. But a lion will not back down except to another lion, and we have *a lion—the* **lion of the tribe of Judah, Yeshua,** *and he will destroy the satanic powers that attack the people of God.* "*Trust in the Lord with all your heart and submit your ways to Him and He shall make your paths straight*" (Proverbs 3:5-6).

I hear all the time, "Ms Scotti, you don't know how the devil has been attacking, and I can't help myself?" Really? You don't think I get attacked, too? You are not the only one, and if you are under attack, stop retreating into your hole of oh-why-me-oh-my-I-am-going-to-die. Stand up; where is your armor? Could it be you haven't worn it in quite a while? Maybe you don't even know where it is. Shame on you. Trust the Lord, get that armor on, get into the Word till you are set free, pray in the Holy Ghost. The devil hates that because he doesn't understand it. Submit yourself to the Lord and he will take care of you. Stop whining, pick up your sword of the Spirit, and start using it to cut down vain imaginations, to silence the voices of demons, to destroy the pestilence by night for He will take care of you.

So what does Paul tell us to do? Put on the full armor of God so that when the attack comes, you will be able to stand your ground.

I met a young lady a while back who was battling depression. I love her testimony because it shows tenacity and the love of God. I am not talking about the kind that says, "I am sad today." I am talking about the kind that says, "I am nothing, I am a lost soul, and I can't find my way. Death would be a great escape, maybe I will cut my wrists because this pain is unbearable. Maybe I will take a few pills to deaden the thoughts in my head." Only the enemy comes in like that. I saw her heart, how sincerely she wanted a touch from God. We prayed for her, and I continued to pray for her daily as I knew that I knew God would deliver her. I didn't know God's full plan, but I knew He would heal and give her joy, and she would be the mouthpiece of the Lord. Her testimony would set thousands free, and so it was perfectly clear to me why she was having such a hard time. The enemy wanted to kill her because he knew her testimony would damage his world.

One Sunday, I remember she came to me for prayer, tears in her eyes but still in faith. "I don't know what to do," she said, "I think I have done all I can, but nothing is changing." Oh, how I felt it for her. I started to cry, and we prayed together. I don't know exactly what I prayed, but I believed God would protect and deliver her as she stood faithful to His call. I know how that feels when you stand on the Word and you still don't see change. You wonder if this is your lot in life. But I spoke to her like a mother hen to her chick. Don't you give up, stay in the Word, pray in the Holy Ghost, and do not look at the circumstances—look at Yeshua and keep your eyes focused on Him. He will deliver you. He will never fail you because He has been faithful to me and He is not a respecter of persons. What He has done for me, He will do for you. I stand in agreement that deliverance comes now. Now walk around your house, anoint the doors, windows, and each child's room, as well as your room. Dedicate yourself and your household to the Lord. Speak it out loud, "As for me and my house, we will serve the Lord and only Him will I serve. Even with my last breath, I will speak the name of my Savior Yeshua (Jesus), but I will never turn back ever again. Hallelujah."

Finally, living like victims instead of victors.

It is my opinion that far too many Christians today are walking around wounded in their victim mentality. They say they believe but have no faith in what the Word says about them and furthermore don't know what their rights are as a child of God. Their faith goes as far as life is good, but as soon as something happens that is a test of their faith, they go into a victim mode. They are like children hoping the world will save them.

This is pretty easy to see in our general population. Look at the welfare ranks. They are climbing in huge numbers. Welfare was never meant to be a way of life; it was to be a leg up until you found a job. These days, people aren't even looking for a job—they just want the government to continue supporting them. The system is most certainly broken, but Christians who depend on the government to support them when they are able to work are wrong and go against God's word. Now please understand, I am addressing welfare recipients who can work but refuse to work, not those who cannot work and need some help. Also, I am not speaking of social security individuals who, by the way, earned that money and it should not be given to those who have never paid into the system. That being said, you are a victim if you think the only way you will survive is if the government supports you. Where is your faith? Getting off my soapbox.

Victims always have an, "Oh poor, pitiful me" attitude. Nothing good is ever happening to them and they start saying things like, "Why doesn't anything go right for me? I can't get ahead, I will never be healed, God has forgotten me."

These kinds of people will drain you, be careful. You must change their conversations to the positive. Do you believe God has your life in the palm of his hand? That He has plans for you that are for your good? Do you believe by his stripes we are healed? Again, it goes back to what are you believing? Have you been in the Word daily? Are you spending time with the Lord?

Because this is what God says, "What are you believing?"

James 1:6 says, "But when you ask, you must believe and not doubt, because the one who doubts is like a wave of the sea, blown and tossed by the wind."

Do you believe God will do what you have asked? Do you believe He is your provider? Healer? Deliverer? If so, stand firm don't be tossed with faith one day and doubt the next day because that is why you will receive nothing. Stand firm it is in the standing that we become victorious.

Chapter 7

DECEPTION AND THE SPIRIT OF JEZEBEL

This is the greatest area of battle because if the enemy can get you to believe a lie, you will be thwarted from your God given orders. You will then become ineffectual and, frankly, you will be out of the battle.

What is deception exactly? Let's start there. Webster says it is the act of fraud, or to trick or to mislead.

But today, I want to give you a new definition:
<u>Deception is a lie wrapped up in a morsel of truth</u>.

You may ask why I say that. Because this is exactly how deception occurs. People will sit in services, and if they are not in the scriptures daily and have an intimate relationship with the Lord, when they hear something that sounds good, but is a lie wrapped in a morsel of truth, they bite on the morsel of truth and swallow the entire lie. Here is what the Lord has shown me over the years. People think the enemy is going to be obvious when he comes calling. But I want you to know that isn't how he comes. He comes looking pretty good, well-dressed, learned, and often times his words sound good. Those individuals who are what I call the Bride (sold out for Yeshua and in the Word daily waiting expectantly for his return) are aware of the tricks of the enemy. They hear the words of a minister or evangelist etc. however, sense through the Holy Spirit something is not quite right here. Be aware that sometimes it's just a mistake in delivery, but this is rare. The Bride knows the scriptures and wastes no time confirming what she has heard. Then when it doesn't completely line up with the Word, she realizes this person who delivered this message may not be of the Lord or they may have a Jezebel spirit. Those individuals who have not spent time in the Word may fall prey to the deceiver because they don't know the scriptures or they have not received the infilling of the Holy Spirit.

Now I know there are a few ministers out there who wish to contradict previous statements about the Jezebel spirit, saying the bible doesn't talk about a Jezebel spirit; there isn't any such thing. I say this is true. Only Jezebel is mentioned, but when the church in Revelation is addressed, we know that Jezebel, the wife of Ahab, was not there. What the writer is referring to is the actions and deceptions that are perpetrated by one who is like Jezebel. Therefore, it will be referred to as a Jezebel Spirit or Jezebel for those reasons. If you find fault with that, take it up with God because that is how God explained it to me. It really doesn't matter, Jezebel or Jezebel spirit, we know what it means. And frankly, I think some ministers want to play semantics with what I am saying, and that is okay—whatever makes you happy, you can call it Jezebel or a spirit of Jezebel. Either will describe the fraud and deception that one who is a Jezebel can perpetrate.

> *Revelations 2:20-29 TLV*
> *Verse 20 "But this I have against you, that you tolerate that woman Jezebel," It goes on to say what the penalty of being a Jezebel will be and encourages the believer to hold firm to what they have received until Yeshua returns. Hold fast to the Gospel and we will be victorious calls herself a prophetess yet she is teaching and deceiving My servants..."*

When an individual preaches or teaches something other than the Word of God as a way of deliverance, this person is a Jezebel. In fact, what I realized is that Jezebel in the Old Testament was so deceitful and cunning she convinced Ahab to let her worship her god Baal because she didn't believe the God of Israel. In an act of **tolerance**, Ahab lets her do it. Isn't that what we are seeing today in our churches and nation—preaching tolerance and acceptance of all peoples, and programs even if it is contrary to the Word of God?

So how many are deceived by this type of person? More than you know. I can tell you from my own experience that some of the very elect can fall to a Jezebel and often do if they do not address the problem and remove that person from ministry. I have seen entire families destroyed because the leader was unwilling to remove a Jezebel from ministry. Sickness, death often follow the man or woman who does not obey the Lord and the Word in correcting the problem. This is why it is so important to be able to identify and discard and dismiss falsehoods connected to such people. Look folks, be careful who you let pray for you, who lays hands on you, and what words are spoken into your spirit. Not all who profess to be followers, apostles, pastors, prophets, and evangelists are anointed by God. Some are wolves in sheep's clothing. Jezebels.

There is a trend in the Church that if the pastor asked a prophet to come to the Church, it must be okay. You cannot depend on that in this day. I tell you, you must discern for yourself because the pastor can be wrong sometimes, too. He or she may not see what you see. After all, he is just a man too and is capable of missing it. My concern here is for the people of God and their ability to discern rightly for themselves, and that can only be done in an intimate relationship with Yeshua (Jesus) and studying and reading the Word of God.

Now don't go run up to your pastor and make all kinds of judgments from this statement for there are many men and women leaders that are anointed and speaking the truth to the world. But I think if you are one of those who feels the need to run to the pastor for every little thing you see, then let me say this, whenever you discern a thing, you must take it to the Lord first. Ask the Lord to lead you and give you wisdom and scripture. Then continue to pray for your pastor that he will have eyes to see, also to raise up, others who see and can confirm what you have seen. Finally, sometimes it is necessary to fast. When you have done all this and God gives you direction, then you go to your pastor in love, and again I say LOVE, for what you are about to share will be exposure of an individual or teaching. Once said, it is his or hers to deal with. God is faithful and even if it is not received, God will work it out however He sees fit. The danger then falls to the leader for he will have to answer to the Lord one day. So pray for your leaders, all of them. They have a heavy burden in caring for the sheep.

Chapter 8

CAPTURED AND TORTURED

When I was in the Marines, one of the experiences we had to endure was what to do if we were captured and tortured. Thank God they didn't really torture us, but they made us go through the gas chamber and sing the Marine Corps hymn, ALL verses. Well, I can tell you that it was torture to me. They would repeat over and over, "You aren't getting out of here until you finish." They would command, "What is your mission?" We would respond with name, rank, and serial number, period. When we finally got out of there, we all thought we were going to die, but we didn't. There were a few who didn't make it through that and were sent home. So it is with us during those spiritual attacks that feel like torture. When asked our mission, we should be responding with, "I am a blood bought child of the King, period."

When the enemy captures you through sin, you have two choices—to defect and go with the enemy or give your name, rank, and serial number to the enemy and say, "I will not defect but stay true to the one who died for me."

"My name is _____; my rank is a servant of God; my serial number is the blood of Yeshua and I am a blood bought born again believer. I stand with an army of believers, and we will not retreat, we will not surrender, but we will attack until victory is ours.

The enemy will come at you from every side—finances, work, family, kids, sickness, and even death of loved ones. He is trying to divert your attention and take you out, but you are wearing spiritual armor; raise that shield of faith and state your claim.

Sometimes people die in the fight—sickness and death come. This happens in war, but they will have achieved victory for they stood faithful to the end. My mother had a plaque in our kitchen. When I was a little girl, I would read it daily, and I still have the plaque. It says, "Only one life t'will soon be passed, only what's done for Christ will last." This was her motto until she died. She was a fierce warrior princess for the Lord. Those who knew her saw her suffering, but she was a warrior until the end. I have seen that in so many of the saints who have passed on. Especially a very dear friend Becky who has gone on to be with the Lord but while on this earth was a grenade for the Lord. Blowing up the enemy camps whenever she recovered from the deadly cancer to fight another battle. She was one of the most powerful and fierce warriors of Christ I have ever known. What an honor to have been her friend. It is wonderful to see how strong they remain right to the last breathe. I want to be like that too; don't you? So when we get to heaven, we can hear those words we so long to hear, "Well done thou good and faithful servant."

Assemble yourselves together in the faith.

I know there is a lot of chatter out there about how it is not the church building that saves you, and that is true. It is by faith as we know, but the word says in *Hebrews 10: 24-26, "And let us consider how to stimulate one another to love and good deeds, 25not forsaking our own assembling together, as is the habit of some, but encouraging one another; and all the more as you see the day drawing near. 26For if we go on sinning willfully after receiving the knowledge of the truth, there no longer remains a sacrifice for sins."*

There are three truths here. One, we stimulate each other to love and do good deeds, two, encouraging one another, and three, maintaining the faith till Christ returns to being accountable.

Although I believe one should gather with other believers, I do not think that has to be in a church building to be useful to the body. But I do believe there is a need for a leader, elders, etc. who have walked the walk for many years and are able to instruct and correct those who are new in the faith as well as protect the sheep from the lies of the enemy. Now I know some of you don't agree, and that is okay; we can agree to disagree. I have seen what can happen to individuals who pull away from leaders and elders into their small group, none of whom are mature or called by God to preach or teach.

In fact, I have seen more people deceived due to this, pulling away. I often hear, "Well, I don't have to be in a church to receive from God," and that is true. But you also could be stunting your growth and how sad is that, when God has prepared so many good men and women who could feed in to your life and help you to grow? Next you might say, "Well, I get all I need from the Holy Spirit." Really? I can look at most lives and see how Satan has robbed them in some way or another because they didn't assemble themselves and unfortunately were deceived by someone. Look, the truth of the matter is we need each other, and God uses each one of us to help each other to grow and mature in the Spirit. So whether you feel a church building is not where you wish to be, do not neglect the assembly of yourselves with other mature Christians.

Chapter 9

BECOMING FLUENT IN YOUR SPIRIT LANGUAGE: YOUR SPIRITUAL GRENADE

Recently, the Lord shared something with me, and it was later confirmed in prayer that if you don't have your spiritual language, we need to pray that you get it. I realize there is a great deal of controversy in the Church about the gift of tongues. I want you to know that I get Paul and how he said, "I speak in tongues more often than you, but I wish you did, too." This is because tongues is the secret code of God, and Satan cannot break the code. He doesn't know what you are praying for or what God is telling you when you are praying in tongues. Also, when you are praying in tongues, your Spirit is communing with God with utterances. Therefore, you are praying the will of God without even knowing it. I think that is awesome.

Militarily, we can see most wars were won when there was a code language the enemy didn't know and couldn't break. I think in WW2 the American Indian was used to transmit locations and secret messages in their native language. The enemy couldn't figure out what they were saying even when they intercepted the messages. The same is true in the spiritual realm. Secondly, it is powerful for the very same reason, like shooting a bull's-eye at a target or throwing a hand grenade in the enemy camp.

In order to become fluent, however, you must speak the language daily, and in prayer allow the Lord to speak into you with a response from the Word of God. The more we war in the supernatural realm, the more you will be using your heavenly language. I loved the movie "War Room", but it lacked one thing—the code language of the Spirit. It is powerful, folks, and once you see how powerful it is, you will use it more and more.

Praying in our native languages is fully understood by Satan. Therefore, when you pray, he now can send out his army against you to divert and destroy. Christians who love the Lord but do not use their heavenly language are generally those who come to me saying, "Ms Scotti, I try, I really do, I pray every day, but no matter what I pray, it seems to be thwarted or I get obstacles at every turn." My daughter Michelle was always famous for this. She was always trying so hard, doing all she could and praying God would help her, but it seemed that every time the enemy was thwarting her efforts. One day I asked her point blank, "Michelle, are you talking to God in tongues or in English?" She said mostly in English, but sometimes in tongues. I said, "Well, there is the problem. You need to speak more in tongues; it's your secret language with God."

Remember when you were a child and you wanted to keep a secret from your parents and you used pig Latin? Well, I didn't know what you were doing, but you and your friend understood it perfectly. That is the same with God. You and God know what you are saying, but no one else does. Not even Satan and his hordes of demons can break the code. So do not neglect your speaking in tongues.

I seem to pray more in tongues these days than any other way because we are now in the heat of the battle and the enemy wants to destroy you and your entire family. I raise up our kids and grandkids daily, my husband and all my spiritual family and friends. I tell you, the Spirit of God enters my war room, and there is such peace it passes all my understanding because that is confirmation to us—God has got this.

I bet you cannot guess what God's atom bomb is, or maybe you can. It's the BLOOD, THE BLOOD, THE BLOOD OF YESHUA WHO WILLINGLY TOOK YOUR PLACE AND RECEIVED THE JUDGEMENT AND PUNISHMENT THAT WAS MEANT FOR YOU AND I SO THAT WE COULD BE SAVED AND HAVE COMMUNION WITH THE FATHER AND ETERNAL LIFE. When in the heat of battle, you are wounded, plead the Blood, when your children are doing drugs, plead the Blood, when sickness and death are knocking at your door, plead the blood. Whatever has overtaken you, plead the Blood. Satan hates the blood because he knows what it means and that nothing and no one can stand against nor prevail against it. You ought to shout and dance on that one. Amen? Yes, we have the armor, we have the ammo, and now we are ready for battle.

In closing, I want to tell you that God has given us all the equipment we need to overcome until He returns but unless we use it, wear it, and stand in it knowing our God is greater than any adversary, we will be maimed, hurt, and destroyed. Don't let that happen to you. Suit up, soldier of the Lord, put the belt of truth, sword of the spirit, the breastplate of righteousness, shod your feet in the preparation of peace, shield of faith, and finally the helmet of salvation. Are you ready? Let's make Satan shake in his boots because we are fierce and unafraid. We will not retreat nor will we restrain from engagement. Know this, Satan—you and your army are going to die. Victory belongs to the Lord.

I pray this book helps everyone who reads it, that the anointing of the Holy Spirit be upon every word, may it convict those who are pulling away, lift those who are full on in the fight with their brothers and sisters, may it enlighten you to put your armor on and get in the fight. YOU CANNOT FIGHT ALONE; IT TAKES US ALL TOGETHER TO DESTROY THE ENEMY. Do you really want revival? Begin to unify, pray together, stand together, go after those who are wounded, never leave your wounded behind ,and sound our battle cry loud and clear. Just like the Marines always say, so it is in the Spirit—SEMPER FIDELIS. Deus Te benedicat (Always faithful, God bless you).

WORK BOOK

What part of your armor have you been neglecting to carry or wear?

How has that affected your walk with the Lord?

How much time do you spend talking with the Lord and reading the Word?

What battles have you struggled in? Now that you know about your armor, how will that change your attack in the future?

Have you noticed you are using loopholes to live in the World? How has not wearing your armor affected you in that?

Have you experienced devastation? Did you feel like a victim or victor? Did you stand and believe God had a plan or did you give into the self-pity party?

Have you had a child who has wandered away from God? Are you doing battle for them? Get in your War Room.

When was the last time you spoke in tongues? Do you know that you can and do have a right to receive that?

Are you reading the Word daily that you will not be deceived when a lie is wrapped in a morsel of Truth?

Can you identify the enemy through what the scriptures are saying?

Are you being careful what your eyes see? What your ears hear? What your mouth professes?

Do you believe that the word of God is inspired and God breathed for our benefit?

Have you left any saints on the battlefield to die? Are you willing to pour the oil over their wounds?

Have you connected yourself to other believers whether in a church or group? Are there elders who can correct and guide you in that group so you can grow in the Lord?

Have you developed your own creed or read and memorized the one written in this book?

Have you started to memorize scripture so when the enemy attacks you will respond just like Yeshua?

Do you now understand what a Jezebel is and how it can creep into anybody?

RESOURCES

Rupertus, Wm. Major General, USMC(deceased) "Marine's Rifle Creed", San Diego Marine Corps Chevron, March 14, 1942

Wikipedia, www.wikipedia.com/ Roman Soldiers, Army, Battles, and Techniques.

Christian Arsenal, www.christianarsenal.com/ Roman Armor

www.ingramcontent.com/pod-product-compliance
Ingram Content Group UK Ltd.
Pitfield, Milton Keynes, MK11 3LW, UK
UKHW022223230426
12048UKWH00016BA/1018